Ambrosian
ABSOLUTION

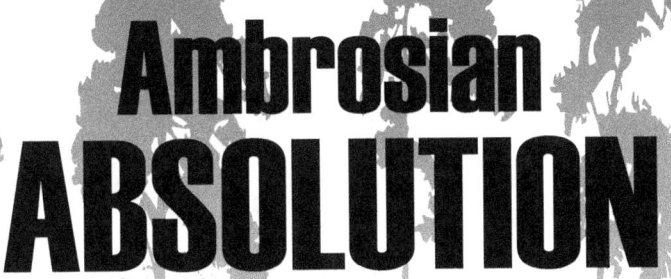

Ambrosian ABSOLUTION

Bel Canto of Love

Steven G. Deaton

ARPress
ILLUMINATING IDEAS
EMPOWERING VOICES

ARPress
45 Dan Road Suite 5
Canton MA 02021
Hotline: 1(888) 821-0229
Fax: 1(508) 545-7580

Ordering Information:
Quantity sales. Special discounts are available on quantity purchases by corporations, associations, and others. For details, contact the publisher at the address above.

Printed in the United States of America.

ISBN-13:   Softcover   979-8-89389-989-4
             eBook   979-8-89389-988-7

Library of Congress Control Number: 2024919069

Dedicated

S.K.O.

In memoriam

William Earl Deaton

October 27, 1928 – May 4, 2001

Never the sailor heralded by land there was,
Who wouldn't forgive the deep blue sea...

Contents

The Overture of the Respectful Distance

I lost the stone tablets.

Misplaced my wallet and keys.

My watch stopped

At a little after three,

My shirt smells like cigarette smoke,

My jacket sleeves like

Dried bourbon from the well of exceptional losses;

There are a couple of debit card receipts

In my pants pocket;

The first is legible but the second

Can't tell the tip amount and the

Signature is a suspect language,

Like some drunk doctor signing for

An invalid prescription trying to impress

The receptionist with his liquor tempered

Academic social graces.

I reach for the aspirin bottle fumble with the

Cap, child and man proof; only one marble rollin'

Around the circle, drawn in the dirt, with the Popsicle stick During an all-night recess in the playground

Of my mind that started with God's blessing

And ended with a couple of notes on a bar napkin,

A stained business card

From some woman who sells wireless air time,

Regionally, hoping for a national position, and anxious

To find the right combination
Of trust, companionship, reliability and danger
She's right and she's wrong about a lot
Of things and about me.
I nudge her to get up, get her things,
She rolls over, covers slide off her thigh
Just enough to let me hear the school bell
Ringing. I look at the business card trying
To match her face to the position
From the dimly lit tables playing host to the rituals
Of man and woman, drink and smoke, music and dance,
Bar bill to wallet, words to nods, smiles to eyes that say
Yes maybe and cabs that deliver the goods.
This isn't her: Fuck, the stone tablets!
There's some kind of distance
Between the recess and the home room of
Playgrounds and libraries. Between whom you promise love
And whom you love. Between what you know
And what you think you know.
You shall worship the lord your God and him only shall you serve
I walked in unannounced. I took a position
Of absolute authority. 1 sat down, laid the revolver
On the table beside the Old one and the New Testament: a gift from
A woman who said it was the only map 1 would
Ever need. She's gone, the blanket hasn't been washed
And the coffee cups don't match, I hear she's living
With her daughter that uses men like
A Chinese accountant uses an abacus while
Hunkered down in the corner eating a bowl of rice.

The one time she opened her fur coat to reveal

The sacrificial lamb of total femininity draped

In pale white silk, laced and scented, La Perla nylon

And garter, elevated by the high heels of pious supremacy

With the knowledge of everything in the good book.

Reveling in the bad one,

I knew right then and there this would never last

But the prayer was answered.

You shall not take the name of the Lord your God in vain.

It happens everyday I try and think of what

It was I said or did to you with you without you.

Everything was too easy, the passion, the lust, the

Desire to rid ourselves of earthly bonds and meaningless

Routines and spiraling cosmic distances at the mediocre

Definitions of self-righteousness spelled out in letters

And words as foreign to religious thought

As is human ethereal passion to spiritual perdition

Speeding at light oscillations

In ordinary time, going somewhere slow,

Nowhere fast. Who is this fucking guy

Shaving me

That thinks he owns me; he's too easy and too hard

On himself. It's God damn madness, that's

What it is, Goddamn madness.

The Sabbath was made for man, not man for the Sabbath, so the

Son of Man is Lord even of the Sabbath.

This is the woman I love who goes

By seven names.

My only time with her is Sunday. She knows what I like

How I like it and how much I like it.

There is no reason for her to think anything different

Or any other way. It was like this in the beginning

Is now, and ever shall be, world without end.

As long as there is a mouth to feed,

I'll feed it.

As long as there is a soul to seed,

I'll seed it.

As long as there is a holy spirit involved in the act

Of conception, I'll conceive it. Sunday is the only day

We have together; her selflessness

My act of contrition

Is worth one seventh the soul of man

Thank god the stores are closed on the Sabbath and she

Wants to believe in me.

Honor your father and your mother, that your days may be long in the land which the Lord your God gives you.

I own nothing. I pay for everything, and it has

Always been true that the father never betrays

The son,

The son will always betray the father. It is written

It is so.

I will sacrifice my son for the

Forgiveness of all worldly sins

But my faith in his life

Will last forever. He. on the other hand,

Will eternally hold what little love

There is to hold.

Against me. Thank god I never had any

Children of my own. I can go to hell.

Spend long days and longer nights in perdition knowing

My father's seed

My mother's womb

Conceived and sheltered me

From the lies and the

Truths

Of everlasting life; my father's name stops with me.

You shall not kill

To give true and meaningful love

Is to kill the very essence

Of the human condition in the world as we

Know it to be. I screamed

For more love and what I got

Was pure hate. 1 put aside

Her will, her trust, her gifts of talent

I robed her spirit

Little by little

Until she told me

Something inside of her

Died.

You shall not commit adultery

Martini for me and bubble bath Fridays

For her

To cleanse the soul and quash the thirst

For more than any two men and one woman

Can bear. She soaked in the bitter water

Awaiting trial and I sat on the floor

Sipping, staring, passing judgment the unorthodox

Kind: an aberration,

An acquiescence of the dominion of monogamy

A surfeit without conscience.

I fought for her

And I won her again and again

Her husband

Won his own battles, they will always be friends,

She and I can only stay lovers;

The one you sin with

Is the one

You will live with, forever.

You shall not steal

I took what wasn't mine to take,

I thought it was you.

You shall not hear false witness against your neighbor

If I told you a lie that I thought

Was true at the time

I told it to you

Then later, realizing it could never be true,

Let you go on believing

The thing to be true for the goodness I thought I saw in you Would I
be bearing false witness

To you?

*You shall not covet your neighbor's house, you shall not covet your
neighbor's wife*

Let me go

To where the flowers grow

To where the wind stands still

To where the stars

Fill

The western slope of the Rockies

Every evening when the sun

Goes down

And I can kneel down beside the

Running water

Kiss the ground you walk on

The same dirt

That will cover my casket

And pray your

Husband never finds out about us.

I walked in on my wife

And her lover once

And it wasn't pretty.

You shall not covet anything that is your neighbor's

I went looking

Retracing all my steps

The night I lost the stone tablets.

I heard the voice in my head

Give me directions

But I couldn't remember where I left the gift.

I walked from the bed to the kitchen

To get a glass of water

And try to think

Had to swallow the aspirin first

Her name, what was her name,

The thigh, the tattoo, the ankle bracelet,

Clues

She said she loved me

I bought the drinks
The dinner was to be fish and loaves
Not some farinaceous bag of mixed messages
Designed to make me envy a richer diet.
This isn't my house, it's hers
There's some kind of distance
Between the rooms
Of love here,
Some kind of distance only
God knows of
He told me what was it he told me?
He told me it was going to be simple,
Simple to understand,
Going to be simple:
The tablets, that's it the stone tablets!
I smashed them last night
In the parking lot the girls thought it was funny.
They thought I was funny
The business card: the wireless airtime, she
Left without me I got into
The wrong car. Like Jesus
His disciples kept a respectable distance
From him
While he walked alone in the desert
Listening to that voice

Questioning

Praying instructing guiding laughing

Finding giving taking and forgiving

Until they were sure

And he was sure

His mind was

Simply

Made up.

Bel canto of Love

I killed a small dog

Once

While praying in the sacred precincts

Of the desert mosque in

Saudi Arabia.

I tied one end of a short rope

Around

The dog's neck

The other end to a large rock.

The Muslims trek across

The desert sand in search of Allah

The most Merciful

The Beneficent

Ended at the well of my camp. I dropped the

Dog and the rock

Down deep into the well

Of non-existence

Sinking in the water of sorrow.

There is a name

For nothing without you.

It is 'me'.

I turned from the well

For want of understanding,

Speechless, my companions

Of the blazing fire

Left the warmth
For shelter from the Empty Quarter
Of desire
I stood alone for almost
The entire night
While the crescent moon
Chasing Venus
From horizon to horizon
May have inspired Mohammed
To keep his people in the desert
Dilemma of trust
It did little for me.
1 dropped the dog
And the rock
Without remorse
But with total Christian empathy
To the one
Who would truly be free
From all of this.
If I were to die
In search of
Another
I would want it to be this way:
A mightier hand then mine
Takes me
To where the struggle for existence
Without you
Is weakened by the
Rope and the rock of

The most merciful
In the well of sacrifice
In the water
Of sorrow
Let me go in belief of a God
And the
Last day
Of judgment.

The Art and Confusion of Familial Desire

In both speculative biblical and presumptive Darwinian terms.

She is a spiritual and realistic mix of the two Mary's.

One to whom you praise her children

One to please the more controversial

Temptations of the Christ figure (To ensure survival

Of the species)—Just before

He died for her and her sins.

I look at her

And 1 succumb to an overwhelming

Desire

To pray to someone or something,

About something or anything I'm not familiar with: either release me

Or

Never let me go.

Isn't that just like the scriptures? The two Mary's,

One

Troubled and

One graceful:

Blissful, ethereal and earthly tormented; they are one.

She says:

"Isn't the truth easier than all of this?"

Truth like

Impressionistic art: I can be a mirror to you for a better life,

If you believe what you think you see

Or

Realism: Love is a
Spectacular catastrophic collision
Of one deal gone bad and one deal
Realized.
Love is the two Mary's
Of biblical truth and realistic
Speculation
Of innate familial desire all rolled into one
Captured neoimpressionist Cenozoic moment;
Confusing and beautiful
To the eye
Of the beholder:
Release me, but never
Let me go.

Strike the lake with a Sword

Compromise or sacrifice?
Does a man compromise his being
For love
Or does a man
Sacrifice
Everything for love?
Compromise or sacrifice:
I was in love
I am in love
I will be in idol worship of love,
Love is the essence of my being.
I have given this thing about us
A lot of thought. I know what it is
I see in you: my youth.
I always thought of myself as young
At heart, restless with passion, adventuresome,
Curious with love and full of life.
I gave you all of me: all I know that
Is true of me.
But something inside of me has died.
Something that was once so big
Is now so small and empty.
I know now what it feels like to
Grow old, I know now what age
Feels like. I will never be

Young again. I am
Compromised or sacrificed?
I am bumping into
Distorted mirrors in the hallway maze
Of self-inflicted horror.
My mind is light speed in the quagmire
Of shattered glass; no coherent thoughts,
No complete sentences,
No river phoenix.
I believe in nothing except you and
I lost that to compromise.
I live on the center stage of perfidious applause.
The light shinning on me is the one light
Lost to darkness
Just before the moon excuses the sun
Like
It is the light of a candle burning,
Dancing silhouettes of unspeakable drama
Across the perdition of criminal trust,
Just at the instance of apostasy,
When the breath of God
Releases the flame from the wick.
There are only empty seats
In the theater of love. Everyone
Is an audience of one.
Clapping, thundering, crying,
Everyone of us an actor,
Auditioning for the part,
So to speak,

Of immortality.

We are cast

Adrift in the philter lake of God's tears,

As dead sailors would be

Returned to the sea

Of one solution:

To sacrifice.

I do not fear sacrifice.

I fear the razor edge

Of my sword

Pressed to the cheek of God.

I fear the temptation

To strike the tears of compromise

In the holy water of sacrifice.

I can not stand any nearer

To him

Or

To her,

But I will lose her

To inimical immortality,

In the instance of apostasy.

I am the other face of God:

Not grace not beauty,

But pain and suffering

In the name of love.

They are of the same ethereal lake

And I must raise my sword

Towards the tears of God,

And

Strike

Like the soul of the river phoenix

Released as the flame

Of compromise from the wick,

Risen,

Again young

With pure love

And faithful

Sacrifice.

The Woman who dances in two rivers

The water at your feet
Runs in two directions.
Down from the mountains
Into the fields and towns
To drink
To nourish
To feed the soil, cherishing the earth
That gave birth to life and love
To the oceans that feed and nourish
The sky with clouds to return the water
To the mountains.
You dance in two rivers;
One of life
The other of love.
You take from the mountains what was a gift
From the sea, waiting, knowing
What flows in one direction
Will return from another,
Like your dreams to thoughts
And your thoughts to dreams
One becomes the other
The other the same
Like when I ride from the ocean of clouds
To give the mountains
The waters at your feet

Or

When I hold you in my arms

And kiss you

Like we are two-calypso lovers dancing

Where the two rivers meet.

The Cowboy of the Clouds

La Mujer que baila en dos Rios

El agua en pies

Corre en dos direcciones.

Hacia abajo de las montanas

En los campos y pueblos

Para beber

Para alimentar

Para alimentar la tierra, abrigar la tierra

Que dio a luz a la vida y el amor

A los oceanos que alimenta y alimenta

El cielo con nubes para volver el agua

A las montanas.

Usted baila en dos rios;

Uno de vida

El otro del amor.

Usted toma de las montanas lo que era un obsequio Del mar, Esperar,
instruido lo que fluye en una

Direccion volvera de otro,

Como sus suenos a pensamientos

Y sus pensamientos a suenos

Uno llega a ser el otro

El otro el mismo

Como cuando cabalgo del oceano de nubes para dar las montanas

Las agues en pies

O Cuando yo lo tengo en mis armamentos

Y lo besa

Como Somos amantes de dos calypso que bailan
Donde los dos rios reunen.

Ei Caballero de los Nubes

No one has ever seen God

You leave me
Lightheaded from Fridays kiss
Slightly wounded
From Saturdays wish
I know where beauty begins
It goes on
Beyond the wind
I've seen the place
Where rainbows end and all
The colors blend
Into hues and dreams
Captured and released on biblical paper.
On paper?
Face to face
With you is like being
In a room with John
For his testimony to the true light
For just a few minutes you hear
He is not the light
But God gave him the light
And
You
Have to believe what you see,
And him,
And me.

Believe in Me

The morning of the crucifixion of Christ,

Two days before the resurrection of life,

No one could possibly have known at the time

About the pending salvation,

I was drunk with determined spiritual masturbation

Alive with sacrificial melodramatization

Dead with no melodious compass direction

Sober in mendicant perdition

And confused as hell.

I didn't return any calls that day, even though I don't recall the phone
Ever ringing,

For fear of being recognized for what I am;

A Captain and a devil in God's own self-ordained foreign legion.

I skirted the edge of town looking for

A state-owned liquor store

Where truck drivers do their best

In the worst of situations,

Unnoticed.

I didn't notice

All the telltale signs of the foreboding nature

Of things to come. I was too busy

Spinning around my compass rose

Like there was no magnetic field to slow the

Disorientation of love.

I had been up all night, walking, because I left my

Domestic Queen by way of lese-majesty

And lack of devoted celibacy;

Unattended, scorned, and with faithless everlasting lesion.

She burned my letterhead

With contempt

And I hers with a perfidious match.

I was courting the Bean Queen:

Queen Susan The Coffee Lady of Medford.

The Royal Queen of Portland decrees:

Fuck you. Fuck you. and Fuck you. Steve.

NO MORE PERSONAL CONTACT

Requested, warranted, or wanted.

I was tossed out the side of the helicopter of monogamist tranquility
Like a Viet Cong guerrilla that won't deliver

Any military secrets.

I was on the skids, knee deep in Deuteronomy,

Ass-wipe deep in spoiled kempshee

God Save the Queen.

God Save the Queen.

I do remember looking skyward

After I tripped in a small crevasse

Trying to avoid a coiled snake, garden variety,

But it frightened me nonetheless.

I looked up and saw the blackest clouds I can

Recall ever seeing. Once when I was trying to

Fly out of Kissimmee I saw some very black clouds swirling

In from Miami

I thought it might not be a good idea to take off

But I was heading north and west and if I could get off

The ground in the next 15 minutes
I would miss the aim of the lightning bolts,
It was as if they were rooting me out, random at first,
Then narrowing their search, then exact and determined.
I left Kissimmee to its own devices, and I was sure
I wiped, or smeared all my fingerprints.
That's one of the good things about the airplane,
They can outrun a pending storm if you have to leave town
In a hurry, otherwise there's no necessity to fly,
Only luxury.
Jesus, I was told, believed in facing the truth, head strong,
Not afraid to fly, but preferred walking, into the storms.
Some one wearing a Copenhagen baseball cap, carrying
A brown paper bag twisted around the neck
Of a bottle of Kentucky blended bourbon
Held the door open for me, I said hey thanks, looking
At his Vietnam veteran and proud of it tee shirt, he said
Did you hear they just nailed ol' Jesus to the cross this morning;
It's a crying shame after all he tried to do for his country, his people,
Damn they took it all away
From him, and just think, he's out there in a field just
A few fucking meters from the airport, well gotta go deliver the
goods.
Naw, its news to me I said and I wondered why Jesus just
Didn't board a plane as I slipped past this guys
Southern hospitality and lonesome tired eyes. I was
Looking for a martini without the ice and the vermouth.
I wasn't really interested in the guy, both of them;
The vet at the door of the state-owned liquor store, or the kid

On the cross that missed his flight.

My head was reeling with misunderstanding. My allegiance was

To the flag of Portland, my faith to Medford, and Alaric wasn't
Answering his cell phone.

I just cheated on my wife. Well, I thought I wasn't

Really cheating and she isn't really my wife,

But we both live like she is. I have a trouble, I've been trying

To blame my problem on the Army, with commitments,

The intimate personal kind. If I can prove I was a different

Person when I was drafted into service then I am

After release,

I can start drawing some sort of disability pension

Or receive vocational training

Commensurate with the civilian job force,

To ward off the awkward effects

Of a failing economy and my place in it.

I fly for this bottom-feeder 'one phone call away from folding'

Cargo operation based just outside of Disney World,

In Kissimmee.

I can't really bad mouth the operation,

Hell, I work for them, they didn't recruit me, I searched

Them out and faxed a good paper resume to a

Shyster skyster owner and he took advantage of me

And my needs; he pencil whipped a background check, said my

Past was crazier then the present and it would take to much time

To figure out who I really was,

And offered some very surprising low pay in discontinuing amounts

If I would just show up on time

And leave on time; deliver the goods. I wanted my down time

To be my time so I could try and write this book,

So I shook his hand.

He gave me an airplane and a co-pilot and pointed me

North and west, told me to call him if I needed any airplane parts,

Otherwise, stay off the fucking phones or I'd be charged 35 cents

Per minute, deducted from my direct deposit pay,

NO MORE PERSONAL CONTACT

Needed or requested or wanted.

Alaric, the Visigoth King, who would eventually go on to be the

Conqueror of Rome, around 340 years after the death of the kid.

Use to be my first officer. He went on to better deals, I took the

Mail run from Portland to Eugene to Medford and back, daily.

Six days a week, three point five hours of flying in a thirteen hour

Duty day the rest of it writing. I get e-mail from Alaric saying he

never

Forgot the things I showed him about flying

The airplane and wished me luck on the book idea, he wanted to be

Mentioned.

He said he even passed some of the flying techniques learned

Onto his loyal subordinates just before he got resurrected and

Sacked Rome. That's the last I heard from him. until two days from

now.

I'll bet he got laid a lot. What with a name like that and all.

Most girls just want

The promise of burning down the town

When you land

And taking them with you

When you take-off.

He could deliver the goods. That's what I remember

The best about him; delivering the goods.

So I purchase my vodka, imported formula from Russia,

Bottled in Hood River Oregon sold just outside of

Medford consumed in Portland at the displeasure of my Queens.
Grieved by my lover who is convinced she is only

Second best. I have the next day off, so does the kid on the

Cross. Who knows what Alaric is up to? I walk across

The empty parking lot, which was full of eighteen-wheelers

Just a few minutes ago, they must have gotten the word

That the last stretch of highway,

Between death and resurrection, was clear of state troopers,

Put the pedal to the metal so to speak,

And got the hell out of Medford,

Not fifteen minutes before the lightning storm

Would start the forest fires still burning a hole

In the federal budget. Breathe, dawg, breathe, secondhand smoke

Is more lethal than the consumption of one cigarette at a time.

It's hard for a politician in times of trouble

To rectify deficit spending, they can justify it,

But they can never rectify the loss; only try to salvage some good

In the cosmic realm of damage.

So it was with me, a politician of spinning love. I threw valuable
resources

On the flames of desire,

But forgot to check the account balance, the tortured, the troubled,

The sorcerers and the soldiers, the lame and the blind, all lost faith in
me

In the smoke-filled valley of the twisted politics of carnal desire and
true love.

She was worth the spin, she was not, the compass rose of true love

Was rotating

Out of control.

She was hope restored, she was faith destroyed.

I was drunk on depressed love and intoxicated by lust and greed.

What was it the truck-driving Vietnam veteran told me? Proud to serve?

No, it was that news about the Jesus kid. I tossed the bottle of vodka

In the parking lot refuge receptacle, which is another word

For last chance salvation, and decided to drive

By the Field where he said the crosses and commotion were. Sure as shit.

There they were. There were a couple of people milling around

Mostly unsure and despondent, kind of kneeling and sitting

Around the foot of the cross. Some of the older men were

Trying to get the young body down before the clouds parted.

I rolled my window down to yell something at them

But the wind and the rain stopped me from saying something

I wasn't sure if I should say at a time like this,

No one would believe me anyway so I rolled

My window back up and headed back to the airport.

Nothing I could do about it; it looked like the damage

Had already been done. Same as me.

There was a lot of static discharge in the air, made the radio

Station that plays soft rock hard to listen to, what with the crackle and all,

So I pushed the scan button

And got bits and pieces of easy listening, country classics,

All talk radio and interference from the northern lights, raging

From the volcanic like sunspot eruptions and the threatening

Shower of meteorites dodging the once in a lifetime

Close alignment of the planets, visible at dawn only if you

Look in the opposite direction using a mirror and a piece of cardboard,

Preferably white, with a pinhole through the center. Its official they said,

Jesus is dead on the cross. Protect your eyes, your vision; we cannot
Count on him to restore sight anymore. That's all the announcer said
Before he played some oldies but goodies, I think it was 'Stepenwolf'
'Get your motor running, head out on the highway...'

It all reminded me of the day Princess Di got killed by the drunk
Security guard while trying to escape a night out on the town

Discovered by the envious paparazzi. They said her head was smashed

In the car crash, but where was it, really? On the head rest or in the lap

Of her midnight dance partner? Her family wants that kind of information

Withheld

From the public but Jesus, we sure want to know everything about

Mary.

The investigators went so far as to inspect the moment of conception

For the poor dear, and the only thing the people said,

Who were in or around the room that night,

Was 'It wasn't me! Musta been the fucking spirits! Yeah, dats rite bro,
Dah fucking spirits did it, dats rite, dats how I sees it!'

That's it, and they wiped up or smeared their fingerprints, the scene

Of the crime is immaculate! This is gonna be a special baby.

Destined for greatness in love, and premature death in life. He's

Going to create the whole damn mess of it all, that one, with one little word: Love.

Glory on High.

I'm confused.

I'm a registered Republican but I don't vote. I just accept the voter turnout

And outcome

And live with the everlasting political spin.

My dream is the one the kid spoke of: Love.

Only they killed him

Before I noticed him or got the chance to fly with him.

I could have showed him what I showed Alaric

About flying in and out of the clouds.

In and out of danger.

In and out of high- and low-density traffic areas

In and out of combat without getting hurt

And he could have showed me a thing or two

About getting in and out of a lot of things like

Commitments and shit like that.

I was too busy with my airplane, my loveless Queen and

My Queen lover. I should have paid more attention to

The voter pamphlets and the presidential debates on television. They said

You can fuck a Queen if invited, but you cannot fuck with

A Queen unnoticed, moreover, two Queens, one on each side of

A Jack-of-all-trades.

Not me, I saw debate with no solution with the Portland Queen,

And salvation and resurrection with the Bean Queen. I literally fell in love

With the right proposition, the wrong hand for the troubled times.

In the politics of persuasion and

The exercise of message therapy, that kind of politico compromise

Can be career ending at best, or get you severely dead at worst.

But I got my airplane on the ramp

Just a few meters from the spot on the field where the people

Were bringing down the crosses. I looked up at the sky and

I saw the black clouds of Kissimmee remembered

Looming over the hills of Medford and I felt my

Stomach turn for the worst and my head was reeling from

The message I received from Queen Bean the Coffee Lady

Saying 'You fucker, fuck you, fuck you, fuck you,

Don't ever come into my airport or drink from my coffee stand

Again, as long as you live and I hope to God that isn't much longer!

In fact, die now and burn in Hell forever!'

NO MORE PERSONAL CONTACT

Needed, requested, warranted or wanted.

What a way to go. Even for the best of criminal intentions

Of delivering the goods, I was wrong to shout love

Into someone's ear without first

Checking for earwax, or a clog or plug or some kind of protection

from

Perfidy; the breach of faith.

All I had to do was to deliver the goods, like Alaric can do,

Speaking of him;

On the morning of the resurrection two days later, I get this

Picture post card in the mail; Greetings from Oregon,

And I'll be damned; it's Alaric in a Copenhagen baseball cap standing

In front of a flat bed tractor trailer with a load of timber logs destined

To be little Mexican crucifixes for the masses of mourners believers

and

What-if-er's already knocking on his door, he has this tee shirt on

That says Proud to serve, and he's holding

What looks like a garden variety of a snake stuffed inside an empty bottle

Of Kentucky blended bourbon, weird I thought, I couldn't

Tell for sure, what with the bottom part of my progressives steamed up.

All he wrote on the back was Hey baby, slow down on the Martini's

And limit the shots of espresso to socially acceptable suggestions. No one's

Winning here unless you

Deliver the goods. How's the book coming? Best of luck,

Sorry I had to run the other day, it wasn't the looming storm,

It was the open road sans state troopers. Leave the coffee bean Queen alone, her providence domain is restored with her own faithful. Your King and indebted friend, Alaric.

P.S. She's already cool without you; it's the Officious Queen of Cool Conception that

Requires your immediate and immaculate attention.

I've always had honorable intentions at first

Then something eventually happens wrong at last:

Love, the sudden and premature death to the gifted ones.

It's our time. It's our world. We must proudly serve

The King of Wisdom

And the Queen of Dedicated Hearts, it's the only way to stay calm

In the face of the looming storm.

Queen Bean told me that before the conception could be ordained

Immaculate, like it never happened,

She could never believe in me again. Queen Dorothy had her own

Reason. She'll never believe in me again.

The magnetic variation at the latitudinal and longitudinal coordinates

I was standing on was too great a margin of error to correctly

Distinguish right from wrong between the two pole Queens. I couldn't Fly south of emotion for the winter

Or

North of logic for the summer,

I'm either in Madagascar and can't pick the flowers, or I'm in Alaska And can't fish or hunt. I was screwed blued and tattooed, backed

In the corner of the penile penitentiary isolation ward stripped for Suicide watch pending the sincerity of my maladroit confession to the

Officious Queen and my acceptance of the maledictory decree

From the Bean Queen.

My fingerprints are all over this crime scene

And no one, not even a jury of my peers or even my boss, the Shyster Skyster, no matter how close to Goofy he is,

Would take or hear my case.

The only thing I can do with his cell phone is dial a prayer, run up the bill

At thirty-five cents a minute deducted from my direct deposit, which would be the insult to injury and then it happened:

Insult to injury.

The company phone rang I said slowly 'hello' and the spokesperson, a Major, for the US Army said Steven, wait I said how'd you get this number, and he said Mr. Deaton, the Military Department of the

United States believes, after

A careful and thorough investigation and analysis of the data collected

In reference to your claim for benefits and or rehabilitation vocational Training based on the fact that you claim you are a different person now

Then you were before you entered the service, that you are in fact and Nature that very same person aforementioned and you will continue to be the said same person.

You asked to fly, we taught you. you flew, and we let you,

You could go at any time; you stayed, when we asked you to stay longer,

You left without a trace. Sound familiar? You've always done that. Even

In puberty, which is before the draft age or very near too it. Ask any of

Your ex's, before and after your tour of duty. Case closed.

The US Army's official position regarding your claim for benefits and or rehabilitational vocational training is one of denial.

We regret not informing you sooner, unfortunately one of our networks of

Global spy (investigative) satellites experienced some atmospheric Disturbance after then sudden and untimely death of the kid on the cross

Sending shock waves of disruption

In both the multimedia and all personal forms of communication.

Not everyone could send or receive proper messages during the

Short period of catastrophe and chaos. We can only try to justify

The turmoil this static discharge may have caused and officially Apologize for it,

But again, the Military Department will not be liable, nor can we rectify any

Damage done. Sincerely, Major O-fish El Satisfaction.

NO MORE PERSONAL CONTACT

Requested, warranted or needed.

The calm and the storm; the divine test to see who will stay, who will run,

Who will walk

And who will fly that's all there is, a divine test and no study guide

(Remember, the bible hasn't been written yet, we're still trying to figure out why the kid is on the cross between dealing with our own issues and those of the ones we love we hardly have time to comprehend his ordeal)

You can't take off from one city and land in another,

Day in, day out, six days a week,

Without eventually twisting an already confused pilot,

Especially if he enjoys espresso with a twist.

His King sacked Medford

His Queen hammered the wooden cross pieces into place

In Portland

And is holding onto the three nails left,

One for the ankles, two for the wrists, just in case

The airplane doesn't leave the Medford Airport on time.

On the third day I'm going to give that airplane

Back to Kissimmee

And start walking again.

That's what happened to that kid, I think. He ended up not

Having anyone to talk to. He tried to leave town

One two many times shouting love and looking for a home and damn

If enough folks didn't start to believe in him; the younger,

Less than immaculate Mary was even ready to abandon

Her chosen profession for him

But he had to deliver the goods NOW

She said, like me, I think he was going to do it.

I think he was trying to

Deliver the goods but his discontinuing amount paychecks started to bounce.

There was

Just enough folks who believed in him to cast a scare and

A higher then normal voter turnout that confused

The politico into thinking enough was enough to justify
The crucifixion of him but as we can clearly see, they can
Never rectify the loss of it; the love thing misgiving, ever!
Life everlasting,
Amen.

The dull edge of a compassionate knife

Liters of sacrificial blood

Fill the waste bins of ruined love.

The floor is stained

With soul to ceramic tile

Grease from the detached garage of despair.

The walls close in on the rising

Tide of tears

Shed for everything and nothing

What's so ever to do with

Us anymore

But everything to do with you.

My wrist is cut

With the dull edge

Of the compassionate knife

Left in the kitchen drawer near the corkscrew

Of twisted love, especially for this

Moment and my mind

Is lost to the grief.

I cannot see clearly past

This small room I'm in,

The body of the Madonna

Violated

Lay lifeless beneath my sink

I am on one knee

Beside the truth

Looking over my wine stained shoulder

At the cell phone

On the dinner table of compromised communion

And the operator

Is repeating a plea

For more information and someone

Is on the way and I can't remember

Where I've been

And I reach into the drawer

Wondering

What knife will sever from my soul

A selfish man's unimaginably

Sorrowful

Coveted sin?

Pico de Orizaba

I was loved by you
Like God
Knows me too well:
It is his ritual
Of a slower suicide
That attracts a despondent soul.
Not the illusion
Of another prayer unanswered.
So let it be like
Genuine concern for love for us,
Not like idiot compassion for life.
Let me make the dead
Live again,
Let my god be a slave to sin.
Let's
See if he is
As God as me:
There is a dimly lit room

With a crucifix nailed above the door
Just across the southern border
Of every human heart,
Where just one peso
Will get you a bath;
Two pesos
Gets you bathed.
'Take the two pesos deal' you cried.

The Caballero of Clouds and Wind Swept Changes

Over the Western side of the Cascade Mountains
The morning sky looks as inviting
As any autumn roundup with the promise
Of pay dirt
And a long drawn out high stakes poker game.
The clouds roll across
The prairie of uncertainty in lesser moments
Of guilt, with ennui,
Like tumbleweeds playing tag with nirvana
In the adult playground of laissez-faire.
I descend into the Rouge Valley of Need
Like smoke from the Biscuit Fire,
Roll'n over the sky caught in the Pacific wind
Of air to breathe disguised as an accelerant
To confession
Or a witness to confusion, either way, freedom
From nine months behind bars,
An ignorant reminder of
The most costly of all flames in recent memory,
Burning the hills surrounding
The promised land of a one road town,
Like Earnest Tubbs stepping towards the microphone
Of love songs on the first stage
Of 'this life will never be the same again', or

Like hunting down relentless the one
Who killed my only family: my brother
And his young wife with child.
I start howling lonesome words
Worthy of humming along like Los Lobos
Sniffing' his mate across the rapid river bed of impatient
Tomorrow's,
Under the full moon
Of slim chances,
Setting southwest behind the ocean
Of thoughtless self-absorption,
Yet rising on the limitless outback
Of genuine earth tone colors painting Australia.
One side of any town
Can be well lit by popular opinion the other dark as
Any ethnic hell.
I walk towards pending outcomes
Like a tinhorn wrangler skirt'n Sunday Services
With the saloon of improper gestures
Closed for repairs, the general store restocking
And the Sheriff is sleeping in, I see
Most folks are sing'n hymnals but a few of the folks
Are down by the river fish'n and prepare'n
For the annual town picnic.
No one seems to be holding any grudge today
So I'm pretty well safe from sticks and stones
As long as the pastor don't single me out
For any kind of personal testimony or
Some of my unprotected back wages. He's reading a letter

Found near the entrance to the Apple Gate, under a tree,

Seems I dropped it by mistake, awhile back,

Just before the will of God and

The Lords' own sacrifice

Mistook my message of any reconciliation

To make us all one.

The letter from the patron saint of precocious clouds,

Tantamount to wind swept changes.

To the bathetic Roman gold exchangers

I carried, was to remind everyone

Of the four or five commandments

That earnestly pops into their minds

Every so often as to make them think

There couldn't be more to it then just that.

(No one in the Valley of Sure Bet Fog could be sure exactly If there had actually been Ten Commandments written or spoken

Or whatever, or just four!)

All the letter said was just owe nothing

To anyone except love, to the one who loves another

Has fulfilled the law.

That's all there is to the word, that's it.

Ain't nothing wrong. I just been thinking:

Someday this valley will be spiked and riddled

With them there train tracks, there'll be more dang people

Roam'n the town then there is good drink n whisky

They'll be drive'n the price of tobackey up

And talk'n to east coast bankers on things

They'll call 'cell phones' they carry in their

Saddle bags, replace'n good ol'fashion prayer

And companionship.
They'll be able to walk up to any
Sidewall of the town bank, day or night, and the popular currency
Will dispense at their convenience and one or two
Of them will own a new fan dangled thing
Called a 'flashlight',
Let'n'em think they can see in the dark, like God's own
Private forgiving eyes.
Darn it woman, don't leave me for one
Of them; they'll never see the light
And the glory of your love; they believe this life's
All about money.
They're damned to the solitude
Of rougher conditions and stress levels
That would make the rising rouge river
Of perfidiousness envious.
I long for that third ace drawn, that reprieve
From dusty cattle drives
And dry throats
And
That private room upstairs
Scented with your new Sears and Roebuck perfume
And decorated by your fancy dress.
I hang my hat and pistol
On your bedpost, sweep you up in my arms
And kiss you
Beneath the stars not yet named.
The idea of settlin down
Away from the battery-operated afterglow

Of the real campfire in the hills

Surrounding this one road town

And chew'n

Some private fat

With you. it's not a biscuit in memory of.

But the bread and the wine

That

Would make for a nice eve-nin and lend

Promise to that full moon

Of gentle cowboy persuasions

And a sunrise

Of peaceful Indian like surprises.

There's an old oak tree

Down by the creek, been there longer

Then wishful think'n, I dropped a love letter there, once,

I reckon the tree will be there

Provide'n shade and comfort to us all

Long after we pass our most precious time

On this land.

Bury me there, before everything changes for the worst.

Or worst yet, for the good

I wasn't born to see,

Beneath that tree

Down by the creek,

With a copy of the good book in one hand,

And a portrait of you

In the other.

My only other option save the Immaculate Conception

A ship drifts away from the dock
The train pulls out of the station
A car backs out of the
Driveway
The plane pushes back from the Gateway
The buses stop driving
And the cabbies are
All on strike and the phone
Was never answered.
Too many people
One too many lovers
Are saying goodbye to one another
I'd prefer it the other way
A ship sails into port
A train arrives at the station
A car rolls up the drive
A bus makes it to its destination
And a taxi claims a fare and you
Catch the phone on the
Second ring
And the Cafe Bella Union saved
A table for two for us
If you have to think about love
You haven't loved

If you have to question this love
You don't know what love is
If you must doubt my love
You have never really
Understood a true love
My thoughts, my questions, my doubts,
My love, has sailed the seven seas for you, has
Lumbered down the tracks of here and there
Has climbed to higher clouds has hungered
For a ride across town in an urgent manner.
The pure pleasure of love, the reward of our love,
Is exasperated and exalted by the perditions
Perception of torment. We live in a world
Not unlike
The one who lived and died for all our
Sins in order to bring
The kingdom of heaven
A little closer
To earthly providence.
Spiritually, my only other option with you,
Is to wait at the table hours days and nights
I taste the bread, which is his body.
I drink the wine, which is his blood
I do this in memory of him: He that has
Given up his body for life everlasting
And shed his blood to cleanse our souls
To give us a deeper meaning of love.
But I hunger here now for you
I thirst

For one chance at love one moment of glory
One kiss of excited arrival
Not a hopeless embrace
Of a tender goodbye.

The Essential Truth to Athens

I am searching for the most romantic
Cafe to celebrate your arrival
Only now, I am discovering this city
Is overflowing with round table peace treatises
Composed to displace the battle of the sexes
From the mundane routine to the excitement
Of the sidewalk cafe then to the bedroom;
Day in, day out.
It is the frappe with sugar and creams
That is the negotiating device
And the crowded sidewalks
That draws each other near.
Each cigarette butt that fills the ashtrays
Set at the tables mark the intervals
Between wishful thinking and concessions,
Each frappe; an offering.
So far, I have only taken mental notes
Of some of the best places
To represent our individual positions: EgoMio Cafe,
Cafe Society, Wall Street Cafe, just to name a few.
I am trying to first visit them
With you.
Our first European purchase must be a pair
Of designer sunglasses; Faconnable.
You are not modern if you cannot sit

With your eyes seductively hidden
Behind the dark glass of mystery.
The clue to youthful Greek sexuality is written
On the label of your outerwear.
Style is introduction,
Accessories are foreplay,
And conversation is intercourse,
The kiss climatic to be sure.
Oh, how the Greeks can kiss in public places;
The treaty is signed, sealed and delivered.
I am so cool, well, not quite. The finishing
Athens touch to coolness is, of course,
A lover and a mobile phone.
It is the most fashionable thing to be
Sitting at the table with your dark eyes companion,
Straws bent at thirty degrees Celsius
From the cold frappes in anticipation of warm lips
And all the while both enjoying
Each other's company
But expressing your passion for life, love,
Work and play in animated conversation
With someone else on the other end
Of the satellite hook-up.
One of the funniest things I've seen in Athens
Is the rush to be somebody
When a phone rings at a sidewalk cafe.
It is not the phone that rings humor,
But the sound of all those glamorous accessories
Jingling

As the entire crowd sounds 'schuzay'
While they reach for the stars.
Who will be the lucky one?
Everyone watches and listens, while trying not
To be at all concerned
With someone else's fabulous fortune
To be discovered by western satellite
In the crowded fishbowl of public envy.
One answers the call
Like tuna turned shark
Signaling the school of coral colored
Bottom suckers
To take another puff of their
Cigarettes in cosmopolitan style
And all negotiations begin again.
They fill the air
With the smoky seductive incense
Of self-righteousness and desire.
The pace of the search for love quickens
And the restlessness of Greek conversations
Turn bent straws erect.
Style, accessorize, converse, listen, enjoy,
Ignore, see and be seen, puff
And suck, I love it here:
This place called romance. The essential truth
To all this cafe intercourse, of course, is this:

We can be anywhere at any time
As long as we are together,
Come soon. Let's see and be seen in
Romantic splendor
Let's EgoMio swagger.

Baptisms for the Dead

We were swaggering
High spirits
On the second day of Police Bureau
Orientation. We were going to
Be Portland Officers. Coats and ties
For the swearing in ceremony
And a walk about town for a sandwich
Couldn't slow the excitement.
I stood on the corner
Of anticipation and anxiety
Asking myself personal questions of
Faith and doubt, the essence of service
And the commitment to sacrifice.
This young woman literally
Rounds the corner and falls into my arms.
In the pale gray light
Of the midday overcast,
She's dying, turning blue. Her girlfriend
Runs right by us, panicked, crying for help.
She screams her friend is choking
On lunch. I have the girlfriend in my arms, she is as
Soft and blue as I imagine the line
That separates the sky from the Mediterranean Sea
To be. She is on the horizon
As far from me as I am to you.

I turn her over and whack her back

Between the shoulder blades

With one swift blow her roast beef

Blockage is cleared. Her eyes drift towards

Mine as I lay her down on the concrete

And she sighs a lover's sigh

Of foreboding disappointment and certain surrender

I see her soul escape thru

The disbelief of constricting pupils

And she dies. I put my hand on her cheek

And with my thumb I part her lips

And lean over and kiss her goodbye.

I blow my breath with the promise of forgiveness

Into her mouth and again

I try to convince her to come back to me.

She hesitates like

A woman compromised should

Her eyelids flutter, her lips quiver,

And her mouth gasps for release

From all of this. She breathes.

I brush her hair from her forehead

And I wipe

Her last lunch from her cheek and chin

With my hand,

The blue of warm water

Turns lighter as she

Struggles upward, she whispers something

From just below the surface,

I place my ear to her mouth

As she lay

On the only sidewalk that has meaning

In this City of the Particle,

She succumbs, says: "I love you."

She is the Doric temple of Athena on the

Ruins of the

Acropolis of life.

A virgin in the Parthenon of my

Guarded tomb overlooking the sea.

And the ambulance driver takes over

I am pushed back

And she is given oxygen

And her weak pulse is taken

And her friend and her are swooped up

By the siren attendants and the flashing lights

And the traffic is separated

For the urgency involved

To perform their duty

And she is driven away from me.

This other recruit looks at me and I look at him

And we shrug our shoulders

And we walk inside the

Building

I have dirt on the knees

Of my Meier and Frank slacks

And part of the last supper

On my tie and coat

And my hands are sticky

And the taste of her

Surrender is on my lips

And on my mind.

And in an hour or so later

We are sworn in

As Portland Police Officers.

I am lying in the sepulcher

Of disillusionment and abandonment of dreams

For more than seven years and I

Cannot see the absolution from all the

Wicked nights and

All the crooked days and no one will

Entertain me or attend to me

Or claim me

So I walked away from it all.

No siren, no flashing lights, no acolyte

No gun.

But I cannot breathe still

I cannot be a Police Officer anymore.

I cannot save lives nor can

I take them.

I went to extremes

In both directions and I wound up

On the lesser side of the middle

Of everything.

I see right past everyone

And into the void of commitment and compassion.

Standing still,

I face nothing

One sidestep to the right

I become mediocre

One to the left

I am breathless.

Where I'm at I can grasp

What little faith there is to salvage.

The strength to move the rock

That seals the burial caves is a gift

From a higher authority

Not a proud possession

So it seems.

The resolve, the power, the commitment

Comes from somewhere else, deep

Inside the breath

Of faith.

It rounds the corner of unexpected

Intersections

Crosses streets of undetermined

Destinations

And collides with meteoric precision

On the only place

On the planet no one can explain.

We were borne to live

On the only globe we know, but we're afraid to love.

Love and romance

Is all around us. It is who we are

Meant to be.

It is not a vacation destination

Reserved for pre — planners

Best fares, ridiculously low prices

And friends fly free advertisements.
It is who we are. who we should be.
I was tempted once
To turn everything I know
To be true
Into something I know to be false.
In fact I did do just that.
I preached a gospel of hope
And I acted out a passage
Of despair
I fell at the foot of the alter
Of trust
My life is in your arms, now;
My heart is beating weaker
Then the compromise of union.
My vision is narrowing
And my lips are quivering
There are no swimmers in the blue
Water, I am alone with the deep
And I am sinking
My mind is racing against time
And my presence is slipping away.
I am a coward to struggle.
I am a vicar of hopeless surrender.
I feel you wipe the water
From my face and mouth
I feel your lips
Part mine. I feel the gentle wind
Make white the surface of the

Deep blue sea and I can see the
Horizon that separates the
First from the last kiss.
Before these days were numbered,
I believed that faith could save me.
On the first day
All I said was 'Love'
And everybody killed me,
Like Jesus
Laid in the sepulcher of faith
Surrounded by people
Who know better.
On the second day they worry
About him,
I confessed one Baptism
For the remission of all my sins,
Praying for
The third day.
Looking
For the resurrection of the dead
And the life with you
In a world to come.

The Unapproachable Light

There was this guy who met this girl
In the narrow hallway between
Presumption and serendipity.
That about says it all
Except for a few minor details
That would define
The rest of their lives.
He was married, she was not.
Go figure: in twenty-three years
She would be married and he
Would not.
Now wait a minute: twenty-three years
A union does not make.
Hell, I knew this one girl
That took a lifetime
To figure out what she was all about.
And it was not about me.
I knew this other girl who
Couldn't figure out
What she was all about
And in twenty odd years it was
Not about me.
So, what's so special about the
Narrow hallway between sexual presumption
And the illusion of soulful serendipity?

Exactly this: If you meet the girl,

Greet the girl,

Enjoy the girl,

Surrender to the girl,

Love the girl,

Give to the girl

Everything you can take

Front the girl

Conquer the girl

Then get the fuck

away from

The girl,

Without bumping elbows

In the unapproachable light,

In the narrow hallway

Between

I have to come

And

I've got to go.

Buck'n for a Section 8

Leave your hat by the door
You can't stay here
But you ain't go'n nowheres.
You got some explain'n to do
But I don't want to hear it.
You got what's coming to you
But you don't deserve it.
You can't have everything
But you got it all
You can walk out the door
Right now,
But you better be home early
You can eat everything
On your plate
But save some for me
You can rub a wound raw
But you can't scratch
Where it itches
You can see for miles
But you can't see
What's right in front of your face.
You can
Drink
Fight
Cuss

And fuck

Fly a plane

And drive a truck.

It's the Army way.

But you

Can't manage

Any commitment

To save your life. In my time,

The best invention was the 'scratch and sniff' cards.

They took me to glory perfumed days and

Disconcerting memories of habitual floundering.

The magazines of promise couldn't keep

Up with the demand for expansion.

They had to stop production

At the flower and the fart.

I knew this couple once, married for a long while,

Started to look like each other,

Dress like each other,

Shared enthusiasm for the dog, who looked like,

Well, one of them, they used to laugh at the small stuff,

Like

When the dog couldn't hold it before one of them got home

And dropped some gravy train pellets on the welcome mat

Near the front door then sat for hours by the presto logs

Waiting for the real tongue lashing only he could testify too

If he could talk he would tell the truth about old married couples

And what they do to survive the tedious creepy body functions of

Old crotchety men in Bermuda shorts taking out the

Tin can cellophane wrapped chicken boned hash garbage

For the millionth time and

Their fallen prescription brides hiding appointments with resume experts

Soaking them for all they're worth, on paper, that is. What goes on behind

Closed doors are a rehearsal for thanksgiving next. It's a soliloquy

Of do's and don'ts,

Slams and digs, and dog's are God's own creatures

Designed not to lie and to make the dive

In the pool of you never knew me

For the remote control a sanctuary of

Solitude in the hostile frontier

Of 'I don't give a damn anymore'.

This prescription product-pickled lady, who smells

As old as 409 on-faded wallpaper, in my house

Is all that's standing in the way

Of my rapscallion penis privacy and me.

She says: This old man evaporating in my house

Is all that's standing in the way,

I think,

Of my virginal recalcitrant rage and me.

I was in the Army once, a radioman.

She was in the Army too, a young bride.

The dog was in the Army too. a pup.

Sergeant said: "Men. there's only three ways

Outta this man's Army:

1. Dead

2. Section 8

3. Dead."

Serge says I was crazy wicked young and dumb. Always

Fight'n the wrong enemies.

Hell, I was normal crazy; hot. heavy, young and horny.

It was my young bride and

That damn breadbasket dog

Who got his butt whacked

With a vengeance

With a rolled-up Louisiana picayune paper

That kept me from being me;

Not me.

Goddamn the responsibility dog

That shit's in my house, in my castle.

Under my roof, on my wall to wall,

By my sofa, near my spit shined boots

With my retaliatory wife

Scheming down the hall. Goddamn the marriage dog.

Honey, promise me you won't

Say anything about my

Snoring and misfit winery slurping

In front of the kids

At thanksgiving dinner,

And I won't say anything about

Your bladder problem and hair fallen out.

Kids these days; they don't know

What a good war it was. My sententious medal

Is awarded annually

At the Independence Day parade, flags waving.

Oh, stop it, go on watch your game.

I can feel

My penis move

A little when

The Miss Teenage America contestants wear

The swimsuits near the pool of perverted competition.

Hell, what are we judging? Poise and confidence or

Perky tits and tight asses?

She's only as big as my

31 -inch surround sound color screen,

But to me, Miss Kansas is

Going to take me past

This small Section 8 crisis

And on towards a depleted social security entitlement.

I've got to privately scratch and sniff

Any salacious allotment of small

Awards and sacrilegious sacrifice

To avoid exits 1 and 3.

Hell, my radio doesn't crackle

With enthusiasm

And longing

For bullets and Chiclets,

Aluminum foil wrapped chocolate bars and

Lucky strikes, but,

Fuck it, I won't care, God damn the commitment dog,

He did it again. I ain't dead after passing

Fruit cocktail, ripe olives roast young tom turkey

Oyster and chestnut dressing baked Virginia ham

Chilled cranberry sauce French peas snow flaked potatoes

With asparagus tips Parker house rolls creamery butter, tomato

Salad mince pie ice cream Tokay grapes assorted hard candies

Assorted nuts apple cider milk sugar coffee Bartlett pears

Apple pie Sunkist oranges cigarettes cigars

With creamed giblet gravy and hot

Honey glazed buns while sniffing

Bouquets of desert and urban

Mixed tumbleweeds of earnest remorse, we play the cards

We're dealt

And I'm doing the best I can

According to the rules and the discipline of war,

I have reposed special trust and confidence

In the fidelity and abilities of my wife,

I say:

Honey,

Where's my big easy

Rolled up

New Orleans

Picayune paper

And my

Situational awareness hat?

My disappointment with God

I'm troubled
Terribly so, more then you know.
I have a plate glass window
Between my heart and my soul
Shattered
Like one million soldiers
Killed in their sleep
One million lovers lost
Dead at my feet.
My hand shakes the water
From the glass
Like tremors disturbing
A peaceful lake
Water will not wash away
My sin. Water will not
Drown my pain.
The water will not settle or rise
Water, this water of my mind,
Will only flow
Down
Mountains of faith through
Valleys of hope
And float love through my shattered heart
Like beads of sweat
Through holes in my skin, so many,

So small I cannot see them all

Yet

So porous

I can only watch

My body lose water

I can never drink enough

From the shattered glass

To fill the emptiness I feel

Lost.

I am disappointed

With God.

He said of faith, hope and love

Of these

The greatest is love.

And you would never

Know it by me.

I had faith

In us.

I had hope for us

I knew only love for you.

The water, our water of hope

Of faith

Washed down

Mountains of wishful thinking

Through valleys of confusion

And separation and

Like the beads of sweat

From my forehead

From your breasts

As we laid there knowing

We can never

Fill the shattered glass

Of trust we lost faith in us, and hope

In us, and

I said to you

I love you so much it hurts me

To be with you to be without you

And you whispered

I know you do

And

It wasn't enough

For us

It wasn't enough

To live any longer for

Like

One million soldiers of my heart

Put to death in a dream of conquest

Like one million lovers of my soul

Dead at the foot

Of faith and of the hope they shared

Of the love they lost

Of these three things

God said the greatest is love

And for you

It was fucking too much

And for us

It just wasn't

Fucking enough.

Towards More Complexity

At age twenty,
Having lost a first love
Who I thought believed in me
And not the Vietnam War,
I was disheartened,
Alone,
And I knew I would
Never see my father, my mother,
My sisters and brothers
Again
And I stopped writing home
Because I didn't know
What to say about the whole
Disappointment
And
Confusion
And
My life without a dream
Of love
Was without reason and
I smoked one of my roommates' cigarettes,
Then another.
Then I got up
Walked across the firebase
And bought a pack of Kool's

And a Zippo lighter with my ration card.
I walked out
Past the revetments guarding
Helicopters
Towards the wire
Claiming U.S. Army property
Reaching the short distance
From one edge of my bunk
To fifty yards or so out
Into the
South China Sea.
I stood there
Staring
At the waves
Then North across the wire
At the crude wooden fishing boats
Of Vietnamese life beached.
I couldn't decide
If I wanted to start smoking
Or not
Just in case
I would ever go to college
And try out for the track team.
I used to run a good
High schooler mile: good enough
For third place
In the regionals
And a couple of first place ribbons
At local meets back

When I was a junior and a senior.

I always thought about Jim Ryan.

I read about him

In the paper. He was the first track star

To break the four-minute mile.

He shattered his own record

Of 4:02.1

He ran it in 3:51.3.

I always thought about him,

How good he must have felt

Alone and fast, out front

And sure, he created his own wind.

Because he knew

The world was behind him

Or

Within reach; his for the taking.

How fast can a man run?

Depends on a couple of things:

If you're running away

From something

Or

Chasing after something.

Both directions

Can be equally as fast

Or the same slow pace.

I decided to start smoking cigarettes.

I lit the first Kool

From the pack I just bought

Looked up from the flame

Of the lighter-snapped
The aluminum hood shut: zippo style.
This Vietnamese man, from the
Beached boats was walking
Towards the wire and me
Without invitation,
Without reason.
His head and face
Covered by his low tilted straw hat,
Hands at his sides, kicking sand.
I shouted to him to
Stop.
He kept walking
Towards me. STOP. TURN AROUND.
I put the cigarette
In my mouth with my right hand
Inhaled, DO NOT COME NEAR ME.
Then withdrew the Kool from my lips
With my left.
I pulled the pistol, right-handed.
From my holster
Pointed the barrel
At his heart pulled the trigger, exhaled smoke.
I holstered my
Revolver
And watched the waves
Of the South China Sea
Claim his
Sandy blood lifeless, useless.

I took a drag
Off my Kool
Turned and walked back
To my hooch, my bunk.
No desire
No passion
No life
No remorse with no emotion.
I walked thru the door
Sat at the foot of the bed.
The Vietnamese hooch maid, hard to tell
How old they are, dropped the laundry
And the shined boots,
Sat down next to me
She leaned her head on my shoulder
Her hip pressed
Against the revolver,
Stillness,
Loveless, kindness,
Quiet madness.
I lit another Kool
From the butt of the first
And waited for guilt.
Alone and fast,
I have often dreamt of a
Woman like you.
Poised, confident, beautiful
To look at, soft to the touch, compassionate.
I have stared at you in my mind,

Helpless to emotion,

Hapless to passion

Longing for forgiveness.

Your eyes look beyond

The obvious

And into a man's soul, at his anguish.

Your lips tease

Yet encourage extra ordinary

Dreams. Your kiss; salvation.

You must have been

The same image of a woman

Jim Ryan saw in his runner's sleep.

What he did

Was realize the dream of love.

How he did it

We'll never know

If he was running

Away from something

Or chasing after it.

I dream the dream of guilt, relish in

The wisdom of denial.

I chased after lust and desire

I ran from stillness, truth; afraid

Of being alone.

No one

Came to see me that evening.

No one asked me

If I had seen that man

By the wire. No one talked

Any talk about it. I waited,
I wondered what it would be like
To own a car and I asked
Someone how much they cost.
My roommate told me
About one thousand nine hundred dollars.
He told me girls dig
Sports cars, convertibles, red ones.
He said
If I owned a red convertible
Sports car
I could win over any girl
I wanted.
We smoked cigarettes
Every night for the rest
Of the year;
Flying helicopters in combat
Talking cars, home, family, things
To do on a Saturday night, what
It would be like
To get any girl we wanted,
I was a miler, going the distance,
Only difference was
No crowd
No applause
No excitement
No finish line, no world record.
One day the run was over, it just ended.
And I flew home

On an Army chartered airliner.
At fifty-one
The distance I have covered
On a quarter mile track of life
From the first time
I read about Ryan's dream
Until the time I loved you, until now,
Is immeasurably long. I have been
To the other side of the
Locked door
At the end of the hallway
That starts just behind
The eyes
And reaches deeper into the soul
Of deceit and pain
Then the limitless imagination
Can conceive, waiting.
I have seen your face in every picture
Hanging on the walls of every room
In every house
Near every bed I have ever
Sat at the foot of.
I have twisted and turned
Love into lust
Lust into love
You into someone else
Someone else into you; waiting.
I told you once
You have made me feel

The best I have ever felt

About myself

And I was running

A world record pace for you

Staring down the last straight away

Towards the finish line of anguish,

Torment and the dream, STOP, TURN AROUND,

When I heard the shot fired.

I felt the wave of

Despondency, of guilt

Wash over my shoes.

I fell to my knees in the

Red sand of self-absorption and

Total abandonment

Turning back the water

Of the South China Sea. DO NOT COME NEAR ME.

I looked east

Towards home and I will

Never know my father, my mother

Is so far away

My brothers and sisters have

Children I have never

Known

My pack of cigarettes

Fell from my hand

I could see the ocean claim

Them as useless

As me.

I see your face

Eyes crying

In disappointed disbelief.

The want of escape

Chases your dreams of love

Into the despair of a reasonless reality.

I thought I...

I thought you told me

I could get any...

I reach for the wire

That separates the good

From the evil, the lies from the truth

The chase from the escape

But my eyes close DO NOT COME NEAR ME echoes

Across the canyons of miles

Dividing

Mountains from shore, shore from sea,

Man from woman from family.

My last dream

I dream I'm driving, lighter than one thousand nine hundred dollars,

In a red convertible towards home

And I can win over

Any girl I wanted...

The tears from your eyes

Washed down my cheeks
As I taste your salty lips
Like the last wave
Of an ambrosian absolution
Claiming me
Like guilty red sand
By
The South China Sea.

The inevitable act of contrition pusillanimously

As it was in the beginning

Is now

And ever shall be: Guilt

In the name of Love.

I have betrayed my father's love and I have

Loved a woman like

No other love imaginable

To any one man in court,

Least of all me. I am

Defenseless

In the draft of her sensuous deposition.

I am

Weak

Of will to take her as my own.

She belongs

Only to one man in the image of

A God.

I bow in her presence

I kneel in her court

My eyes lowered to the floor

Which awaits

Ever present

For her slipper and the brush

Of her lame robes.

She haunts my life

With her gifts.

I am not a God. I am a prodigal son.

I am lavish

With her desires

I am reckless

With her passion

I am immoderate

With her heart

She has emptied me of reason

For reason

And I devoured

With lust her soul

My Medford Monroe.

She is my union of pain and of pleasure,

Of love and of sorrow,

Of righteousness and of guilt.

What man would not

Fall, what man would not stand

Still for her? I gave her me. She gave

Me her. I could not stand still

In her presence

And I had nowhere to run. I fell,

All of me, in her arms,

And at her feet.

My father, my father forgive me.

I hurt her in ways unimaginable in the name

Of love, like you.

I am less then this in your eyes. I cried for your wisdom.

I struggled for your strength

I prayed for her union, I ignored you
I denied your presence in her, through her
And with her.
Now hear me, pious jurors; Sentries of love
And understanding. This simple life is a simple
Play. But once the curtain falls, the
Words cannot be undone and the voices of actors
Resonate forever in the canals and castles,
Cafes and bedroom of my mind spinning
Time and promises into one useless man
Falling.
This woman; named Susan by man,
Blessed ethereal by God.
Kissed me and stopped my world from orbit.
I am chained
To the floor of self-righteousness
I am thirsty and I am weak
In her cave
Of oblation and of remorse,
Spinning in a merciless world without end
I have only myself to blame
For serving as her God,
Facetiously,
And I starve
For your words, dear father, of absolution,
And the blessed whispered cry:
I love you.

The Cruel and Wise Times of D. Elizabeth LaClair

How should we know love?

It lasts and doesn't last

Fill'r up, endless drives of pain

The summer's best movie

With unknown stars,

How do you do it; without gold?

So hard it hurts

Guaranteed Results

Now you can own it

Unaffordable Payments

It's not so fast this food

Stay in touch

Gratitude, Affection and Honor

Let the dust settle

I recognize pain

Will Portland ever see us again?

A part of my life never touched,

You have your way

In the arms of light

Under the olive tree of dark jubilee

Why do you ask a

Stranger fortune of trust?

A terrible thing in your eyes,

Many paths to one last thought:

Agreeable or not

This is it, Love.

She was wise to leave me

She was stupid to go

On about her business like

Some autumn wind in a

Spring fever, she is not here long

Enough to make a difference in love.

And no one will be the wiser.

I have often thought about

Suicide at the likes of her

But I have maintained a posture

Of indifferent melanoma. The sun

Will take its own toll

On fair skin

And the moon will hollow

Out any fears of love by many people

In Saskatchewan

Of ever finding peace with forgiveness.

We can all take a lesson from them;

Never trust your soul to another

And never believe in

The self-righteousness of childless bliss while

Searching for gold
In a silver mine.
I am forever troubled
By all of this madness
And that is just the way
It is panning out
To be
Between her and me.

The Insane River

She stopped talking
Long enough for me to hear
The snap of her fingers,
Register the wave of her hand
Across my stare into the deep blue doorway of departure...
"You're drifting away..." she said
"You are not listening to a thing I say...you're
staring off in the distance..."
I was thinking about
What it must feel like to
Rob a South American bank of
Carefully stacked and wrapped bills,
Small denominations, no sequential numbers,
No dye-packs, non-traceable drug cartel laundered
Cash, no one makes any sudden moves,
No one gets hurt...
I wondered what
It must be like to
Swim as a dolphin, intelligent
Sounds and smooth gestures, where space
Is real and full of unexpected surprises,
Like getting caught in a tuna net
Under some
Foreign trawler, like being the prince of fish
And ending up

In a six-ounce tuna can

Destined for mayonnaise dressing

Between two slices of wonder bread

Spoiling in a playground lunch box,

Uninteresting pauper of cartoon comparisons,

Swimming where the law of the sea

Is questionable and the

Fishermen of necessity are pirates,

And someone will reach for me,

Through the doorway of departure,

They always do, just after payday,

To stock the pantry with cans

Marked 'dolphin safe, packed in water

Makes them feel good about the coming week towards the end

Of the month when

Bottom fish becomes a legitimate dinner...some

Packed in water...not thinking

My whole life I've been

Slowly drowning...

And with any sudden move

Someone

Will

Get hurt.

In the fall of the Sorrowful Distance

If only for a brief moment
Of our precious time alive, I held you
In my arms and kissed you; I gave everything to God
In prayer
From the glory of his light
To the shadow of our sadness;
The last kiss lingers
Like
A sailor on the misty pier
Of a Philippine night alone,
Dark lipstick anchors
His soul under the cold green sea
Of the pea coat, collar up, and every
Cigarette stare
Across the distance of thought
About you makes eyes water
And quiet madness, an insidious virus to reason,
Drowns prayer
In the sea of the sorrowful distance.
Every wave of disappointment a sailor knows
The sea regrets in the most
Unforgiving ebb and flow of tides.
I will never be the same
Of all that I am or all that I pray
To God to be
Like our last kiss

In the narrow straits

Between presumption and serendipity.

If you never whisper my name again.

If you never allow me to see you again,

Like the hoary nights of November

Alone in the Philippines,

I will understand.

I will stand on the misty pier, longing for you,

In the fall of the sorrowful distance

Wherein

I fell

From Heaven

To Hell.

Hardly a need for suicide

Nothing
Knows love like the rain... It begins
For us
When the rivers find solace for being
Without reason.
But the planets
In heaven
Wait for something,
Still, quiet,
Beyond rain clouds,
Believing,
Like us,
Anything good will happen,
Patiently,
Like time in China.

In the arms of light

The scent of the back of your neck
Lifts a dream
Like a young girl waving flowers
At some man walking
In the distance of a New Haven
Country road
While the sun looked
The other way from the moon
And the spring breeze
Chased carnal wishes in the arms of light
Through open fields of thought
I stood still
Looking, thinking
She should put her hat back on and
The sun should be at the back of her dress
Forever and
This could be
The one day some author of
The bible
Spoke of.

Ambrosian Absolution

When the airplane

Is cruising just above the lower clouds,

The ones that cause the people below

To think a gray day

And the engines are in perfect harmony

With each other and with the wind

And the early morning sunrise

Warms the cold metal cockpit,

I turn my attention from the dancing needles

In round dials

And gigolo switches tempting on or off, adjust the volume

Of my headset

To a cut above sinister level, I smile a crooked smile

At the crackling noise and the steam floats

Off my coffee easier then lifting love off my shoulders.

The airplane is going places and taking me

And my companions with it. We are headed towards

The Pacific at sunrise. The low clouds are

Hanging onto the Willamette Valley for dear life.

I can see the Ocean ahead and it is glorious, still

And waiting. I have often thought back at other

Pilots, at other times, on a morning flight such as this. Those guys in their

Bomber jackets lifting off airfields hidden outside

Of London

Single takeoffs and lofty formations

Burrowing the tops of clouds like farmers fields

Of surfeit glory and thundering Clydesdales unsure of the work ahead

But mighty in the thought of harvest. I surrender to

The flight but I conquer the wind. Those other guys

Flying towards Germany may have thought the same things as I:

The easy vibrations and gentle ripples

Of my mind guide the plane to manifest destiny.

My co-pilot. Curt, is quiet,

Focused, doesn't smoke cigarettes and only has a cup

Or two of coffee in the morning. Not like me. I drink it

All day, especially in cruise flight when Curt is trying so hard

To keep the airplane straight and level. He's young

And capable, I see trust in his eyes.

I distract him for a moment by looking at him until he

Can feel my stare and he turns his head from his instruments

And I give him the thumbs up and he sees my

Crooked grin and he knows something

Good will come of all of this and he relaxes his shoulders

But never loosens his grip on the yoke

And this airplane is commanded to him to fly

Me and my father's ashes out to sea.

I laid down beside a woman

Once

And I remember her; she made me feel the best

I have ever felt about myself

And when I touched her shoulder and quietly moved

My hand along the countryside of her back

And she rolled over just enough

To command me to continue down
Towards the foothills of promise in the Willamette Valley;
She gave rise to another meaning of love,
I told her everything and more.
I was sure of it, I was sure of myself.
I told her that when I touch her
My insides feel like I'm flying
From London towards Germany. My airplane
Is just above the fog and the clouds
And under the light and the glory of God's
Only son
And the engines are in perfect synchronization
With the wind and each other and
With love.
I told her that and she hung on every word
For dear life like the fog over the Willamette Valley and she cried
Like a woman does
Who has been compromised by time and by promise.
But this day, this hour, this flight
Will end soon
I signal with my hand to Curt
To ease the power back and let the plane settle down
I pour a cup of coffee from the thermos
And lite a cigarette.
My father and I sat on his back yard patio
One day holding coffee cups and lighting each other's
Smoke, He said he wished he had time
To move near the Ocean, but he loved the view
Of the mountains from his retirement house and

That was good enough. He loved how the sunset
Changed the colors of the sky and the way
The Three Sisters Mountains
Looked; but never a sailor heralded by land there was
Who wouldn't forgive the deep blue sea. He told me I made him
Feel good, what with my flying and all. He thought highly
Of me, the Captain, the pilot.
I told him I was sorry I never stayed
Anywhere long enough to give him grandchildren. He
Smiled a crooked grim, sipped his coffee
Stared out at the Mountains named for women turning blue
From the approaching dark, and said he didn't
Expect that from me. What he wanted to see me
Do is exactly what I have become.
He said 'Steve, You were meant to do something else,
There is something greater or just as great out there
Waiting for you.' He pointed towards the sky
That invites you in
Touches you
Gives you breath
Gives you life
Gives you faith and hope
As you fly out over the ocean of love.
He made me feel good about myself.
I set the coffee down
On the floor beside the Captain's chair
Gestured to Curt
To bank the airplane gently
Towards the light on the water glistening

I took the ashes of my Father

From my flight case

Opened the side window

Made the sign of the cross

Touching the forehead of the sky invited

The chest of the swelling ocean of love promised

And each shoulder of compromise

That woman laid her head upon

And

I put him out to Sea.

Optical Illusion

Clear head

I am sitting at the pole

And the outside of my car is

Celebrated with promotions, and waxed so bright

And the number painted on the door means

Determined winner;

Like my own questioned wind,

I am quiet.

On the Flattop of the USS Enterprise

As the deck boss signals

The catapult is cocked and his eyes

Turn towards the open sea

My hand is on the power levers

The other the stick

I breathe through the mask with controlled intensity

At Cape Kennedy

I am on my back looking

Towards the heavens

And the launch command

Commences the countdown at ten, nine, eight...

In African heat

I am a tiger free from envy, still,

And I am staring down an angelic gazelle

Grazing in the distant mirage of God.

There is a moment devoid of commotion in the

Absence of choice. Even the winds of change
Whisper cool calm seconds before the definitive storm.
I feel what love is
I feel what light there is in love, my mind
And my body are at peace with the quiet wind,
Choice has been replaced
With decision.
My knee feels the dirt
And my thumbs and forefingers are stretched
Along the starting line and my eyes
Rise to the distance of the track
Laid out in front of me
I have a gold chain around my neck
And it swings with the fall
Of my shoulders as I exhale fear
And inhale concentration;
On the chain
A jewel a tiger's eye from Thailand, the medallion a claw
From Cambodia. I wore this in my youth,
In a war of another kind,
To protect me from harm and show me strength
To endure, to win, to focus, to concentrate.
I am sitting in my room
Staring at the telephone
My head is clear and my mind is drifting
Towards the heavens
The track official raises his starter pistol to the sky
On your mark, get ready...set...
The deck boss salutes me then raises two fingers

Swings his hand around in small circles then
Points and kicks towards the distant open sea and sky.
The crowd stands and the honored guest
Says Gentlemen, start your engines
From the pole position
I can see the distance
And the mirage
I pick up the telephone
And dial.

XIT

There's only one way
Out of the room:
The pale green neon exit sign
With the E burnt out
Hangs in the deep dark
Hallway behind the
Theater stage in the
Auditorium of sticky floors
Dandruff laden chairs
That hinge on total collapse
In the isles of untold trusts, actors both
Oral and congenial, visual and audible
Palms
Stuck on dried coke and sweat from
Close calls, feet can't move
Swiftly
In the slimy buttery stench
Of shared popcorn catastrophe, destined
For mouths
Never fed. I've watched
This movie, these actresses,
First in black and white
Once in color restoration.
Twice on video
Now I hear it's coming out

In DVD and I'll
Be damned if I will watch it
Again. I can't take the ending.
I know it too well, and I can
Always see it coming
As if I wrote the
Script myself
While holed up in some roadside
Motel just outside of
The only rural town for civilized miles
With less then a pint
Of dull worn out wishes
Hoping some midnight sheriff
Has the master key to the cabinet
Of 'I shouldn't be doing this'
And a little sympathy
For a guy who's not from
Around here.
Floating cigarette butts
Like spawning humpback whales
Caught in the camera
Of tourists who have never loved,
Looks like heaven to me.
I am all that sinks
In the bottle of liquid remorse. Ashes float
Like duped Arizona sailors around the
Gila Bend Notell Motel pool
Who were never put out to sea.
There's more determined seamen

In the small desert recreational

Water container

Of contaminated chlorine

Then the U.S. Navy can allow.

Their separation from

The service

Is inevitable, but still

They can hardly wait.

Guilty theaters are dark and lonely

Places in the heart

Of totality in the soul of divine

Graces, and one phone call

Places you in abstract

Scenes of human weaknesses.

I can look inside

Any moving vehicle

And see the occupants but

I can't touch them

Their hearts

Their souls

Are in perpetual motion

Trying to beat the red light

In the intersection

Of stop slow and go, down the shady side

Of

Pastoral road just outside

The landmark theater of love.

'Walk don't run!'

I scream at the

Sheltered rolling habitats
Of today not tomorrow, zinging
Past tired pedestrian movie goers, eyes trying
To adjust to the electron spectrum
Of streetlamps and headlights.
Fluorescent
All night diners with muddy hot coffee
Won't solve anything
But I feel it necessary
To scratch some sort of a tip
On the Formica counter
Of stranger kindness
Just in case the waitress,
Once divorced, twice dumped,
Attractive to long haul
Truck drivers and young
Scuba divers, mostly people
Totally foreign to me,
Turns out to be God,
And what she thinks about men
Is really gospel
And what I think about
Me
Is just as true.
And I smile a crooked smile
And I think I will not make
It in time to the
XIT sign
That grows smaller

The closer you get to it,

The drab heavy curtains,

Thick with dust mites, brushing against

My shoulders, wrestling

With my coat, like

Every woman I have ever known

Who wouldn't believe in me,

Hung in every narrow

Hallway that runs from

Physical Madness

To spiritual hyperventilation,

Behind the stage,

They separate life only

From the concrete wall,

I push them away

From my center piece companion

Only to hide her

Struggle to overcome fear,

Her hand reaches for mine

It is so dark in here

I hear her say: Steve,

Wait, take my hand.

I think I will

But I think I may not

Be able to find Dorothy in the dark,

But I will. I will make it

To the XIT

Sign

With her in

Time.

About the Author

Steven G. Deaton was born in California on Veterans Day, 1950. He received his bachelor's degree in Political Science from California State University. Chico, 1981. His professional career has spanned from police work with the City of Ashland, Oregon, Police Department and as a member of the Special Emergency Reaction Team with the Portland Police Bureau to 22 years as a United States Army Aviator. While with the U.S. Army, and the Oregon Army National Guard. Steve has flown combat missions serving as a helicopter pilot in the Republic of Vietnam, a combat surveillance pilot in the Republic of South Korea, and voluntarily served as an Aircraft Commander flying a utility cargo airplane in Operation Desert Storm.

Steve resided in Portland's Pearl District wherein he was inspired to write his books.

www.stevengdeaton.com

Other books by Steven G. Deaton

The Reperception of Circadian Rhythm

The Weight of a Suggestion

www.ingramcontent.com/pod-product-compliance
Lightning Source LLC
Chambersburg PA
CBHW071523120626
46550CB00006B/2340